All Aberration

All Aberration

Poems by Terese Svoboda

THE UNIVERSITY OF GEORGIA PRESS
ATHENS AND LONDON

The publication of this book is supported by a grant from the
National Endowment for the Arts, a federal agency.

© 1985 by Terese Svoboda
Published by the University of Georgia Press
Athens, Georgia 30602

Set in 10 on 13 Linotron 202 Pilgrim

The paper in this book meets the guidelines for
permanence and durability of the Committee on
Production Guidelines for Book Longevity of the
Council on Library Resources.

Printed in the United States of America

89 88 87 86 85   5 4 3 2 1

Library of Congress Cataloging in Publication Data

Svoboda, Terese.
    All aberration.

    I. Title.
PS3569.V6A8 1985   811'.54   85-8658
ISBN 0-8203-0807-2
ISBN 0-8203-0808-0 (pbk. : alk. paper)

On my first son

(after Ben Jonson)

Goodbye, Deng, Spirit-of-the-Air,
my joy was motherlove to bear

his five years in hope and now in
grief as sweet as some great sin.

O that I could still catch and hold
him! He would do as he were told.

Not even science could reverse
a simple accident: the curse

of life that will not stick. I say:
here lies all reason for poetry,

for whose sake l promise to love no less
the next child who claims my happiness.

Acknowledgments

The author and the publisher gratefully acknowledge the following publications in which these poems first appeared.

Beloit Poetry Review: "Asleep at the Center of a Continent"
Columbia: "Arbor Day"
Early Morning Extra: "Antique Map"
The Georgia Review: "Dance for the Sun"
Harpers: "Painted with Figures a Million Others Have Seen"
Massachusetts Review: "All Aberration"
The Nation: "Dust Storm," "Each Season Contains the Last"
New England Review: "No Season for It," "Wheatfield"
New Letters: "After You Tried to Strangle Me," "Sonnet," "Wood Cut"
Paris Review: "Never the Moth's Token"
Ploughshares: "Transformer"
Poetry Northwest: "Long Distance"
Prairie Schooner: "As Told to Me," "High School Rodeo Parade," "*Putenga*," "Skinny Dip"
Virginia Quarterly Review: "Barking Dogs," "Family Court," "Fleur-de-lis," "Scouting Locations for a Commercial," "This Is What I Have"

Contents

Part Three

Part One

Wheatfield

You disappear into its rowless height
to where the sun is best, somewhere
beyond the middle. I can't see you
select a head, hold it between your thumb
and finger, wrench it from its long stalk.
I can't. I'm a small girl bored in the car
that sits in a dusty ditch. It's too hot
for meadowlarks. There's only the oil drip
to tattoo out the hours. You taste the kernels.
They're sweet, almost juicy. The whiskers
of chaff stick out from your ruminant face.
You'll spit soon. I become breasted
in the wait, the radio's on, clouds
polka dot the wheat's rhythmic shimmer.

Once I see your greying head over a patch
of rye. I assume you're busy pulling it up,
as it's wild and out of place. I'm
in the front seat now, kneading a man's
shoulder to compare it with yours. Has
he baled hay? I'll examine his chest.
When the grain rolls without any wind,
I suspect your approach, but it's only
a mouse running from a weasel. At times,
the two tails of the road curl in the heat
and come together. It's never sunset.

The car doors open and close like the wings
of a preening fly. I guess you're not lost,
except to me. Only my plow-shaped jaw
and my tendency to strong thighs call up
your fatherly presence. That is, until

my own son stands at the field's edge,
his arms akimbo and his feet firm
as two shoots, and he wants to know
if the wheat's ripe yet.

Kittens

Though the wheat fuzz tickles her knee scabs,
her face is stern as she positions the thermos
like a bayonet. Her mission is to deliver

the lemonade. The field all around overshines
her hair that must be washed by Wednesday,
scalloped into French braids by her usually

clumsy mother who now fishes an ice sliver
from inside her dress front. As the child
swims into the grain, the mother pleats

her brow: the kittens caught in the backwater
now float and must be strained and burnt
or buried. She smoothes on rubber gloves,

her movement perpendicular to the scythe
the machine far off has not put down, the blade
over the father and the open thermos.

Hares, he says. He hates to talk.
Dun and grey speckled, like all things wild,
they squirm in a crescent of uncut wheat.

The girl puts them to her, their newborn forms
writhing against her plum-sized womb,
and the fields bend glossily as she makes

her return. *You're cruel to keep them*,
shouts her mother, hair singed, the yard stinking
and ash sticking to the cherry tree leaves.

Hiding, the girl falls to sleep in the warm barn
under a harness. The bunnies, dazed, nearly green
in the dark, hop out of their tomato flat

and the cat who has been watching streaks for them.

No Season for It

Hand on her knee, she stoops to pull
a clot of hair from the shower's drain:

holiday trim from the children gone
to stock market, schools, affairs;

grey souvenirs tangled with strange
infant-hair, not from her womb. She stares

into the fine web. It enmeshes her.
She trips on it, falls into its snarls:

the son swindles, the daughter's
divorced, no one knows her birthday.

It should cushion colored glass balls.
It should be a net to save her.

She rises from her knees, wrapping
it around her, a shawl of slime,

sloughed skin and one long coil of hair.
Does it warm her? Should she bury it

with the nail clippings or press
it in a book? It tightens.

It cuts like spun glass as she wads
it up to poke it down a hole.

No season for it ever, she thinks,
her shoulders sloping like jack pine.

Arbor Day

You planted trees three times.
For less view, you said, and to break up
the sky. Mornings you hauled them plenty
of water and spoke to each in soft tones.
Prairie dogs, you prefer to think,

ate back the roots; the wind wasn't that bad.
Of course, backing over two with a pickup
didn't help much. But others had whole groves
that took to the sand like sagebrush. The dogs
are out now, hesitant and abrupt, the color

of earth against the sky. Hundreds appear,
bobbing up from their holes. All their eyes
seem to see you. It is as if all at once
the land takes them back again, leaving
the horizon empty, but for the lightning,

branching and blooming.

A Terrible Sonata

I
Tryst

It's not really gothic
the way the boy roams
the family subdivision,
grunting and retarded,
nor how his mother
follows him, hiding in
closets so he thinks
she's not. What romance
is there when the horror
and hero are one?

He leaves dark piles
in the foyer, bed, and back
garden to show his hate
of visitors. He can't be
bathed, except part by part
and then his manliness comes out,
furred and erect, no wand.

He does laugh, but wild,
high and hysterically.
Or perhaps it's she,
warding off his blows,
calling it love.
Who's to know—the relatives
who've moved away?
They phone to hear her sound
so tired, so tired.
But it's her child.

II
Glass of Water

Drool refills it.
Fish and eels pass
his eye, banking
in the troughs
of the bubbles
he makes.

He imagines nothing:
all is present,
past and without
future: mother rhythms,
chips of quartz, oil
spots, glass.

When someone walks in,
he smiles. He doesn't
look up when the glass
is held to his lips.
He's used to drowning.

III
Party

The ass's tail is a challenge
even without a blindfold. All
but the smart one don't get
past turning circles. He

takes the prize, but quickly—
rising pleasure causes seizures.
Who can purse their lips?
The cake's come and the wax

of so many candles frosts it.
Such a big boy. Why doesn't
he want his toys? His hands
in his pockets, he knows what

he wants: that Mongoloid.

IV
Travel

As he hoists the boy into the car,
the father's temples pound,
more in anger than exertion.

His mother pleads: make cow sounds
but he's mute as the trees they pass.
As soon as they check in and find closets,

he starts to shout out the sounds
in his chest. Lights go on
in other rooms. *Almost human*
says one tourist. His mother
honeys his lips to quiet him,
but he begins to thump. His father,

driving-weary, takes him for a walk,
but he wants to waltz. The hotel
yes goes off, the moon rises,

a streak of spit, and they turn,
monster and master, together.

Fleur-de-lis

I'd forgotten about stars,
the only prairie ornament.

As we drink on the patio,
they light his head until

cloudcover cuts them off,
chiaroscuro, the way his whiskers

bank over his jaw after five.
I'd forgotten about the emptiness

of the prairie: that morning
we'd gone in the old Continental

to salt the cattle, to collect
what they had already tongued.

He turned north, spinning the sand
and sage, then cast and north again

on no road. *Here*, he said, *do you
want it?* At his feet, a cowskull,

clean, horned, and with teeth,
the wind ribbing the sand around it

with its little nervousness.
I'd forgotten about how he didn't take

thanks. With a jerk, he hurtles his ice
to the dog in the bushes and rubs

his face awake. *There's another*
if you want it but the skin's

stuck on. It needs a few years.
I'd forgotten my mother's half-

laughable jealousy, how her call
always reduced him to the TV.

In a few years, will I remember
how much hair he had and what color?

Ski Lodge Laundry

The others have hit the slopes,
leaving us at the tearing window,
with the crystals closing its iris,
and the menu-life and the occluding

laundry. She lifts the last, knowing
it doubles like bread when left alone.
I relieve her and her hands flop,
reaching for a cigarette. Ah,

children, she says like a sneeze.
Smoke clouds her features and her frame,
all sweater and heavy food, goes
indistinct as if x-rayed. A wraith,

she reveals that bubbles tight as grapes
line her lungs to her heart. The doctors
lie. Ash falls to the floor; we both
dive for it. Rising, she is my color:

rose, the exact shade of the girl
in the portrait of uncertain eyes.
(I posed for days before the TV.)
Who do I look to? What connects us

is as filmy as child's snot: her own mother
died young, so she knits her symptoms
with some assurance. And I? How do I plait
my crowsfeet? In fear. The drifts against

the door, the enforced coziness that only lovers
long for are a perfect vise: we writhe,

extracting a silence like a stutterer's.
Mother pours another drink; I rush on:

do bears die in winter in their sleep?

After Cows Die

Over a blowhole a coyote
faces off against a poodle
that's burr-thickened
so as to resemble brillo.
Birds have already worked over
the stiff swollen carcass
a foot from the caterpillar
tractor, the most innocuous
grey and white birds.

All night the howling's
disturbed the hired man
as he dresses fowl killed
by one of those two dogs,
preparing to smoke it
inside the TV's guts.

If you wonder whether
the howling's a desire
for domestication, know
the poodle's been thrust
from a pickup at top speed,
his tail soaked in gas
and lit. This blowhole's his,
the grass-eating sand.

Even, you might say, the poodle
is someone's brother, who by day
picks out scrap at building sites,
and the coyote's his sister
who sends him money made off
stripping. The hired man is, of course,

the father. Every now and then
he picks off stars with his .44
to make the noise stop. That's when
you can hear a pickup strip
gears as his wife searches
for the turn in the dark back roads.

Dust Storm

Midday dark, tumbleweeds throw
themselves at the windshield and part.
All land is whipped into a black cloth.
I steer by my sweat.

Islands of steel and glass
startle me into direction.
Don't stop, they cry
from the accordianed cars.
Someone's behind you.

Someone's behind you.
I see nothing but sense
legions, sense that my hands
shake from the rumble of wheels
big as a man. I drive on.

A ghost's eye blinks in the cloud.
It becomes the flicker of a marquee
with a hand pointing to parking.
Under it, a town is, for an instant,
visible. I hear the pant of low gear.

Night had blown in by the time
I left the movie to gape at the prairie stars.
The town's single tow truck hauled past
a steel ball, slowly, too slowly.
I found the car yards from a curb
imprisoned by tumbleweeds
with its headlights glaring
for miles.

Part Two

Never the Moth's Token

From the frank rendering of the sock
to the foot and the hem released
of its fold, with scent marking
the crevices like a possessive animal
who determinedly outlines over
and over the contours of habit,

the love-arms come uncrossed
in the dark night, their cashmere
turning to satin, a mere silken edge,
then the thinnest gauze, flapping
behind the branches with the moon
coming through, only inches from
where thread leaves the swaddling
for the shroud.

The Compleat Angler

Sex is the boat we all board.
It's so unsteady
we can't stand up
or get ready.

Art waves from the shoreline.
Yoo-hoo!
I get harder.
I last longer.
Of course
he can't swim.

He sends the swan
to stir the water
so what we enamor
is no longer.

He threatens:
night will fall,
that will be all.

And, yes, the boats gets
lost offshore and drifts
and we hear his laughter
over and over
the dark water.

Hamburgers and Desire

The carhop clipped the tray too close
so the coke cascaded, ice, brown juice,
on my best white shorts. But the burger
didn't get it, swathed in thick waxpaper.

He tipped her and she pirouetted
on roller skates with ketchup.
We honked and honked:
the burger was magnificent.

Gone, we groped for words beyond
Uh-huh to frame our unspent love
but failing that, we kissed.
Our windshield shell magnified

this outrageousness until
car after car abreast the cement
took up that heat and two angels
bearing silver platters—

our double order—interrupted
honking pure Jehovah.

When the Cord's Cut, Another Begins

Seeded in anger, carried like a welt
on my person, you heard me scream
at the worst birthpart, *I don't*

want you: you, sprung frog
on my belly, sucking, sucking,
connected to me like an apple's stem,

wet and dry and wet with the rhythm
of a bad bulb, you taught me to see
each toe a pig, each fist a face.

But no woman wants such truth known:
how she hated and changed, without
will. These ties can be twisted.

Already I foresee your lover's frame
and me, hollow-wombed and silvered.
I will want you then, having had you once.

By Dawn

We all grasp the bed's edge
as it undulates and cuts a spray.
I'm at the prow, the maiden half-dressed
and my hair's uncoiled to my elbows.

You hang from the boom as the mainsail flaps,
shredded to gauze. Who most
bears the brunt of the baby testing
the hulk's forward progress? His land-ho

sounds long before we smell anything but sea,
sight any bird other than a gull's shadow,
hit only what seaweed slaps against my breast.
No one wins that heat.

The baby re-occupies the deck sideways,
pressing me to you in almost that embrace
that began him. Does he want it repeated,
selfish for company, finding the crew

somehow deficient? No time: the ocean wells up
in his throat, it comes from there, we come
from it, it takes us. Now the boat's broken up,
pigs squeal in the gangway, there's vomit

on the cargo and we're all swimming to shore.
We used to wash up in a lagoon with the surf
miles away and the sea anemones opening
their cushions, but now waves pummel us,

the sand in our eyes hurts and there,
in the wake, rock the dismembered dreams.

Skinny Dip

Eddies pull at my breasts.
From midstream, you are another

blossom, swaddled in that color
of cloth and sleeping, I hope,

on the bed of leaves I made for you.
Is the sand beneath you wet? I dive

to a warm spot, fish-breath-hot.
Almost too deep. I fear

not touching. My milk trails up
like octopus ink as a boat buzzes by.

Don't wake while I'm under.
My fingers, a mile off, beckon

but the broad palm anchors me.
When I hit the air

my skull's bones refit. Fish hatch
and swim away, so as I search the shore

I expect to see you rise from your blanket
and skim over the water

and trout to snap in gladness.

Rocker

That part of the circle that the chair rides
meets its tail in four miles, travels through

the roof and into rain turning back into snow.
Her toes run it. Their spasms fix the sway

to the child's pulse, he whose eyes are wide
and sleepless. She lays her head on him,

making the circle shut them in. That the baby
goes to sleep is not the result of back and forth:

it's the seamless promise of the womb.
To this, her cupped hand over him as he breaks

from the breast is a curve that suggests the world.

Barking Dogs

Early one Hattiesburg night,
the moon hardly dry from
the swampbottom, the beer
already half-gone, and sleep
six hours off, a kid changes
into her tutu and tap shoes
and sings Swanee by the light
of the high beam.

We go wild. Even the baby,
nude as a Junebug, tattoos
out a step. The kid bows
and sings the last verse
to the record cover
of her accompaniment
where sit four dogs
on blue stools in bow ties,

each a coloratura. The kid says
they go to a special school
and only eat honey. Oh, no,
someone uninvited volunteers.
You just speed up a tape
and compose a scale. No dog
reads the notes bone by bone.
The kid cries and runs off.

But we aren't going anywhere.
The mosquitoes revved up
in the few seconds she saved
from speech. What more
for entertainment—a coon
chained to the barbecue,
a quarrel?

Sonnet

Three bursts of birds clear the roof.
How many? I ache to add everything.
I'm on my third drink, mon amour,
you're that late. Yesterday's
story of how wolves surrounded
the car and how you tossed the baby
out to scatter them was

fine but what about the frozen
raccoon I found behind the ice cubes?
We're all sick and exhausted.
It's not your slim red car glimpsed
between the trees that I long for.
It's the running over, the forward
and reverse, the nest from the tree.

After You Tried to Strangle Me

I set out: the story's old enough:
winestains underfoot and that color
around my neck, an embossed love-grip.

The light in my eyes shone gassy
under the copper moon but the stars
were the same: linked as oddly as ever.

Our child ran after me, slowing
my escape with kisses. I pulled him
to my collarbone. Far ahead there was

fire: a boy in a corner of the park
with matches, one flame more blue
than the rest. It was clearly a lure.

Every year where I come from
the swallows take apart their nests,
and a wild horse paws the sandy ridge

thinking to find water. When I returned,
it was to review the color of my bruises
against the dark sunset of your lips.

Family Court

Though the mother does not take drugs
to keep her calm, the father is obviously
placid. The child is the boat they all
climb on, even the guard. This is a saga

about seasickness. The judge begins by
considering the mother's legs as she flips
unsteadily through truth's spectrum,
riding the narrative song of the examiner

to its logical and damaging point.
She wants to scream. The variation
possible in her replies: "Yes, but . . ."
are cornerstones in a edifice

of anyone's construct. Surely
the lady with the scales is scrabbling
on the floor for a lost contact.
When the judge taps his gavel,

wide as a foot, into his palm,
it's a soundless wisdom: sever
the heart and place it on a plate
for the woodsman, uniformed and manacled.

What is the refrain?
When do they all break into dance?

All Aberration

A steaksmell invades my path
but a woman walks by with lilacs
and cancels it. *Spring*, my son
says from his stroller, or maybe
sing—I'm too proud to hear less.

We pass parks and parking lots
where in this season only
the very young don't look foolish
in love—old men behind their trucks
with stumped women, bald and lolling
in embrace—they're aberration.

It's all aberration, my palmist
states, sorting one flame from another
on my hand. I believe him.
Last year my friend was murdered,
bludgeoned by his wife's lover,
his own best friend.

Yet it's the age of sudden death:
at thirty, life's less an accumulation
than a situation you've made
for yourself. The stroller's
losing a wheel, but with a little wire
I make it. Then thirty flights up,

rain on every story and the sitter
extending her arms. My son whimpers.
Even in the best of families.

Another woman drops off her brood,
so like lizards the way their heads turn.

The elevator releases me,
allows my womb to snap
for its contents. Sex
is next. I ruin my chances—
I say: you're too rich,
your fingers move over my hands

like fence shadows over a train;
nothing's been necessary
to you since the Armada.
And so, he's too tired.
I collect my son and start
for home. The rain has flattened

the tulips on the median;
petals splash the dark ground.
As I cross the last street,
a man in a taxi whistles,
taking the carriage as a sign
I once did desire, and more.

Antique Map

Between the two of us was an antique map:
none of Florida drawn in, Africa an island.
The boundaries were faint and often erased;
cherubs blew wind from one end to the other.
You wanted it that way because you had sailed
to the edge before and found only serpents.

Then, disguised as the New World,
I lifted my dress and you saw
that landing was possible,
that the natives were restless
but lacked the taste for blood.
Besides, your powder was dry.

But our scales never coincided:
you were always 1 to 300, while I,
1,000 to 1, waved to you
from a football stadium, your nose hair
swaying in the wind of my shouts.

Inevitably, the pope drew lines
around the world, a census was taken,
mines were staked and territories split.
We knew what roads to take and how often.

Our sextants now are filled with stars.

Long Distance

Her voice shimmers in two thousand miles
of pure light: aurora borealis.
What is there is not there: steam rises
from the receiver. As he listens to her,
he strips her naked, touching the forked places.
He misses her moving tongue—so soon
the radio waves stop their pulse.

Long-haired cattle and Indians almost
Oriental live within the Arctic circle
where he, young, hair on his tailbone,
digs for minerals, eats green meat if
helicopters drop supplies too far off.

His eyes, turned rock-color, search
for specimens in a stand of birch.
They sense shape brown as his mother's
living room rug. Then, treed and shaken
by a grizzly dam, whose teeth, old
as unicorns, stink in proximity,

    the narwhal he helped catch rends the net,
    falls to the depths, plunging and plunging

he throws what he has at the cub.

In her bedroom, the early light
on a lover's wrist, she reads he may return.

Sailing Excursion

Blue and white tiles surround
our hearth, as Dutch an embellishment
as the boats seeming to glide
over the land, as the land
invented only to separate one boat
in the canals from another.

In the foreground, like any good
Breughel, we gather at our breakfast
in jerseys of brown and perhaps
a scarlet shoe, our porridge
doused in milk from a cow so laden
her teats are wooden to our

thieving touch. In this gold light
we smoke, kiss, and say all psychology
is religion. Then the wind blows us
back to the watermaze, so like life
in that we can't turn back. The trees
are few, the horizon close as a hand yet

big with clouds roiled in argument.
Dusk has a smokey wick, as if no more
time is allotted us, prisoners
of a holiday. Where are we going?
We are too young to bother with anything
other than pleasure: Bach draws

the sails. Yet we do dock, as silver
in the fresh moon as foreign money
and with awe: those we'd left behind
to try sex lit candles all along the shore,
creating a hopelessly dangerous tableau,
like love, its proscribed country.

Downhill Romance

Jammed cock to buttock
we slice through the snow
screaming: no moon, no moon.
The gully below blazes with a lighter,
then a cigarette's star.

Just short of its smoke, his legs
cascade into a drift like salt
into the street. I land on
barbed wire and bare rock.
The stopping is terribly silent.

As I rise on my elbows, she drops
her butt into the snow and laughs.
I help drag the sled around her
while she shouts: was it fast?
Once on top, you empty your boots.

Never do you touch me. Even when
crashing is imminent, you don't grab
at my breasts. While I warm up,
your hood joins hers for kisses.
Again she'll wait this one out.

So stung with scrub, we plough
into a bag of marshmallows and then
walk home, following someone's
long strides in the snow, like
spacemen in all our clothes.

I shiver as new flakes spin up
into the streetlight. When you put

your hands into her pockets
and talk of the moon's craters,
I ask: how many could one hold?

Painted with Figures a Million Others Have Seen

Light and dark play on the bedclothes,
blotching the lover's nose and mouth,
a field of birds alighting and leaving:
the TV's on and rumbling. Awakened

by it, she wriggles out from under him:
a body filled with sleep and drink
is as heavy as a dead man's. Her ruff of hair,
reflected on the screen, is mussed

and straight up like a salute over the image
of a man at the door with flowers receiving
the chortles of his woman. She can't snap off
the set yet. She is that woman holding

the posies, her cheek atilt for a peck.
She opens her mouth for the next possible kiss
and yawns. The prone man stirs: *Honey,*
hold the fish. She holds it, reaching

under the covers. His snores rock oddly
with the violins. Soon, to build up drama,
the commercials telescope in staccato style.
She doesn't get out of bed to turn it up,

to hear what the woman says in her sobbing.
The truth is, she wants that river to go
over her stones. She falls to sleep.
Much later, it snows.

Scouting Locations for a Commercial

He'd thought having them along
might make homeowners open. But
she's platinum blonde and the baby
owes nothing to him. No one invites
them up for tea, into their family rooms,
onto their decks. Instead, she kisses
him big in a shady lane, her baby

squalling, a matron pumping down the walk,
looking askance. He's quiet after that,
scouring the streets for the perfect house.
But only round-shouldered garages
and white-frame bungalows rise
from the walks, architectures so
compromised it's no wonder the doors
aren't answered, though the car's in,

the cat's out: they're afraid
of further concession. He polaroids
the yards anyway, fashioning
a panorama of normalcy: rose hedge,
startled cat, combed gravel.
He buys mums, bunches and bunches,
to camouflage a crack in the step,
and sod to carpet a fraudulent

backyard. Parents make their little actors
lie about their age, he says, no child
plays as young as he looks.
She primps. He turns the radio on.
They agree they love the City
and want none of those houses, none.
They don't even buy a pumpkin
to weight her child's window.

Dance for the Sun

Hopi: *We sacrifice to the rain god.*
Sometimes it rains,
sometimes it doesn't.
Zuni: *We ask a shaman to cure our sick.*
Sometimes we're cured,
sometimes not.
Navajo: *We dance all night for the sun to rise.*

Our bodies pool and break
like a moon over water.
I know then no candle
need be lit: when the sun
comes, I will be awake
and watching you. And so

a skin forms over each caress,
turning it into something
to take home: a bottle
of ship, its billowing sails.
Silly as any virgin, I plan
a honeymoon: two palms shaking

from a moving hammock. Why?
No cruelties are set out yet:
curled, skewered and repeating
as in a tray of hors d'oeuvres
from a party that's gone on
too long. I don't worry

that you won't be my lover.
It's an odd knowledge,
a kind of control—like
in the Indian tale, the sun's
tinder's set, its match
is already crossing the cover.

Engaged

The pool past midnight holds
what it should: the moon in all
its organdy, the palm's detritus
and the wily engaged. The pool

accepts that swimming: the little boat
they make is mocking of lapping.
But meant: they want more than
each other. When they pull apart,

she, like a fantail or perch,
scissors over the white as the swarm
breaks on the concrete shore.
Brandy refuels their motion

and the moon pleats into slats
fit for a voyeur. Beyond,
sails shadow the seafloor as clouds
cover and uncover the open ocean.

Transformer

The train circled. You two hid
in the algae trees, slinking

around the plastic rocks, bellied down
to the liver-colored land, getting close,

getting closer until whose finger
grazed the tracks? Who cares:

you both reached the station sticky
with glue, the transformer smoking

and the train: crash! *Daddy!*
But that wasn't you.

You asked to meet him our first date;
I'd have married you for that alone.

When you gave me a ring, he got one too
and he carried the train.

You also had mother and father
only by halves: on the same shuttle:

summer, mother; winter, father.
Anger in secret; cry only on arrival.

Soon he had to have your mustache
penciled-in for school and under it,

a tie your color. Those were the best days,
the last. First at the accident,

you checked his heart, his hand,
took his mouth into yours

for a kissful of air. From blue
to pink he went, pink, pink, pink.

Before the signal flickered again,
he was surely, for that moment, yours.

Plug

The instruments of life on video:
the pulse, breath, brain will shrink
to a single pop of light whenever I say.

I said test him when at three he read
Babar. He hid under my skirt, mum so long
the man with the pointed beard gave up.

*He's warm, Miss, isn't he? His color's
good?* Never mind. I have an hour to decide.
But his turnip head; what the doctors said.

Each night he read the same three books
and I went right to sleep. As parents do,
I peeked to check his chest, its rise

and fall with regularity. That the room
should go quiet is unendurable. Like a god
I decree others take what parts he has and live.

Like eggs his organs leave.

Like a Standard the Soot

and the barbered florists' scent bely
the passing of spring and the bird
on the sill escaping south could be
going north and the sun as it sets
in the city increases its arc, yes,
but which way? Whether that bird
be that same as the one that took grain
from the speckled glass last spring,
that beat its wings *chipchop* when
startled by a child's cry, who can say:

traffic overwhelms its song and flapping.
Still, it goes on into the smarting blue,
past the ashes of some doorless building
and into where a plane suspends its passengers,
each of them given up to the hatchings
of the runway, the shadowed prairie,
the trees reaching for the fuselage,
so much so no one knows whether it's night
or day on landing. Not by a bird's song.

It is said that the prairie soil is sandier
than under the city's swingsets, easier to shovel,
if that's what's done now—and that the city
effaces the dead as well as it does the living,
its jam of stones and bones ringing all entrances.
So brown and white was the field where
a few of us gathered that day, cold in sunlight,
the meadowlarks picking among the bouquets
for furnishing, singing *little one*,
little one, over the new turf, There was not

a boy inside, it was me, it was the other
mourners, it was those passing in cars

making the pavement sing over and over
like wind through waving grain.
As the clouds kept on across the sky
and the plane threaded its return among them,
dividing the birds in its path,
so we go on by accident.

I see the leaves point down now
and the sap strangles in the boughs
and the birds, dun as newsprint, fatten
in silence on the city streets.
Where did summer go? And the boy,
leaning into the flowers at the corner shop,
risking the imagined bees, smelling what
was really water wet with leaves, won't he return?
What grows inside me, dark as the moon
lost behind billboards, prepares,
witlessly, to answer.

Down, Thy Climbing Sorrow

She runs from her tears, the water
that will force the bloom, the bloom
arcing to ecstasy with the petals
tearing the air. But to grieve
is to forget: she fears a breeze

will steal the seed beyond the eye,
beyond the details of shape, color,
shell, so she buries the seed,
unaware it roots in that seamless space,
preparing for a pain not unlike

the emptying of the womb: timeless,
excruciating, unwilled. It is the dirt
of the bootsole: the nut, fern, worm,
and web to which all things turn
and recover. She may as well stand still.

Each Season Contains the Last

—for A. and J. Laughlin

Remembering again how my late son
brought leaves in ragged bouquets
to this bleached light, these wavering rays
now slanted with sorrow, for what reason

do I lunge into this Fall head on,
traveling to a lake mysterious as oil
with its coat of leaves, where hunters roil
the birch with bows in camouflage, drawn

to the stand behind the house? How could anyone
call this harvest, or that, the branding
of the trees with blue tape, designating
them to the smoking hearth? Dun-

hued, the leaves he brought were not
the prettiest, they were the fallen, the first
he could touch along the city's streets cursed
with high-branched trees. Then nature did not

seem necessary: the plants he started
in cups died for light; I threw them out
with the leaves. But now I notice, about
halfway down a slope freshly covered

with snow, that nothing is the same:
that even my steps are half-erased
behind me. Thus, like a deer startled
by the unfamiliar, I see the corn lame

and curling in the field not as victims
of a holocaust nor as a defeated army, devices

to recall myself, but as shocks,
feed for a year of cattle. Is this grim

comfort? Nature continues; it does not pass.

Part Three

New Zealand Silence

A road of shells makes a T in the bus' route
where you get off, for nothing. At its cross
is a pub with a dog patrolling like a Grimm guardian.
There is a sort of silence about the place
because you can't quite hear what crashes
at the end of the road. But you're ahead

of yourself: the mist slicks into heavy rain
and underfoot, the shells turn and turn, sticking
to your rubbers like small children. You get
an earache from the wind forcing water into your head.
Then the rain moves like some sexual curtain
and you see what you thought was ragged sky

is a wave tree-high. A few crows flit against it
like black lightning. The road dips and a graveyard
replaces all that water. Its fences, burnished dark
with rain, hold sheep cropping bright green grass
and calla lilies clumping in Victorian excess.
You enter, as surprised as the dead must be to arrive.

They, of course, are as silent in their lava-color crypts
as the sheep are, dropping their fine beans
in the neat trim. Or is that just what you think:
the ocean, heaping up just beyond, bewitches
all sound, even the ewe crying for the ram to stop.

You go on. The T is baroque in intricacy
where the ocean crumbles the continental shelf.
You can't swim there. You can't even hunt jade
along the beaches where the purplish light
slants down because rogue waves may take you.
But this is what you came for, this violence
that is always inside your head, outside.

Putenga, *Pukapukan for "The Sound of Thighs Slapping Together in Sex"*

All day the women have cleaned fish
in the shallowest waters, and their breasts
are what we've stared at instead of the sun.

Now scales stand on their skin as translucent
as the moon poised over the reef. It's sunset.
They've loosened their nets so the last

of their catch breaks the water with its head
as if to see who persecutes it. They talk
while they wrap themselves in cloth

and the syllables resound like the moment
of pleasure. We want to know these words
and others: the one for the colors that play

over the cliff like an out-of-focus Hollywood kiss;
the one for the shivering of a single frond of palm;
the one for the fading of the fishes' stripes in the pot.

There is a shark in the sky as enormous and as close
to us as the lagoon leaking toward our feet.
We need to suggest our puniness: we are

the palm's shadow, which, in the sand,
has the outline of a crushed roach.
Of course, the shark doesn't lunge at us;

its single eye becomes a hen's claw.
But it could have, intimates one of the women
by ducking a falling coconut. They pick their way

through a grove that leans its white bones
in some desire we wish we had. The lagoon,
no longer stirred by fish, returns to the sheen

of mirror backing, then gun metal. A white train,
almost out of sight, defines the horizon
for one arcing moment then all there is

is the roar against the reef, suggesting more.

Toward a Documentary

Out past the veranda, birds
blacken the fig tree, shading us
from the glare its leaves can't.
But at sunset the birds begin
hacking and screeching for room
until the hollows in their bones
thrum. We can't talk.

A servant steps out, claps
two planks together: a gunshot.
The birds drop off, muted
with the effort of flight.

I've described it: how the nights
were punctuated, leaving out:
how the dust raised by the impact
of the wood made the servant cough;
how after so long he'd slam
the sheets against the wall
for scorpions, then we'd retire;
how we'd make love in the cocoon
of the net and come apart
with the pop of sweat; how, later,
after a snake had bit your hand,
and you knew you wouldn't die
but still sobbed once, long after
I should have been asleep.

Asleep at the Center of a Continent

—from an expedition to the Nuer
who live along the Nile

I.

      Tiik flourishes
a switch over the mud bulls
he made at the riverbank.
They grow huge and move.
      Yet boys deride him:
he has eaten from his mother's bowl.
They say: the airplane will come
and take you away.
      He dreams
he is younger,
sucking the goat's
tit.

II.

An Arab holds a knife to Gaac's head,
the white folds of his jelabia a flag
of slavery. He raises his arm in defense

and it is his uncle, cutting the lines of manhood
into his forehead, six times across the endless
horizon between the ear and the ear.

Women watch him.

III.

Nyalual, his wife, hears drums in the distance:
a baby's heart to her ear.
                                        A dance.
Her buttocks bounce under her cattle-tail skirt,
mimick the latest American beat.

                              The pulse
becomes the pounding of grain; the pestle
is a log driven into a hollow trunk. It fades
as softly as a white woman pounds. She dreams
of a second wife, not too expensive.

IV.

Hundreds of Ret's family dance around him,
raising the dust to suffocate him with dignity.
He tries to rise to his boyhood stance:
one foot to the knee, poised as a pelican,
but his joints ache so.
                              He calls out
to the cows in their own voice, to the ox
with horns curved like the bird's wing,
to the bull bright as the moon's hand.
Together they bellow as a cow is taken
for sacrifice: perhaps someone marries
or someone dies.

                  He wakens,
stirs the dung fire,
feels for his pipe
in the ashes.

V.

The white one, Mebor, lows.

She has slipped her tongue
into the river
and sees her nose
reflected
just as the crocodile
seizes it
and drags her under.

VI.

Rushing out on my hands and knees
through the low door, I say
all the right things in their language.

But Gaac marries me anyway,
with his 100 cows and one rifle.
At the betrothal, my mother does not dance
with the other mothers. She stands
on my discarded clothes beating off
the young girls who take even the hair
from my brush.

This Is What I Have

Crones support her in birth
so when the head appears
she does not topple from her squat
and snap it off.

Women who give birth the same year
are sisters the rest of their lives.
All big-bellied ladies brew beer,
laugh aloud cautiously, dare not
give the child a name.

When the drink bitters,
and the child's eyes open
and the breasts seep with milk,
the mothers throw the first stool
into the river, singing:
*even this small thing lives
in spite of you, cruel god.*

And if the child grows, one night
the grandmother will waken him
to tell tales into the embers
until the old woman's teeth loosen.
One by one, she will give them out
saying: *for you, child, myself.*
This is what I have.

And the child will string them
on the wiry hair of some giraffe
and wear them into age.

Upended Umbrella

The moment the mountain
began paying out road,
the Italian towns
no longer matched the sounds
on the map, not four letters close,
and the car winked with heat
like a hatless farmboy.

Chickens greeted us
at the airtight trattoria.
We locked the car, went up
an outcrop of rock to a church
where an upended umbrella
caught a crack of light
from the sacristy. A dog
looked up as we crossed.

Beyond, a set of white smooth stairs
zigzagged into the vista
where surely someone lived.
Indeed, two kids tore out
of the clematis to tell us
something: we nod, they point,
we follow. They almost dance
in their excitement but then

suddenly leave. We keep on.
In the last twenty steps our feet
sink into unset cement.
We can't ask the workmen folding

kerchiefs around their salami
for directions—or forgiveness.

We stop the car at a bridge
to wash our shoes. The water
runs clear but for fish, handfuls
transparent as lice, sliding
ineluctably downhill, surely
to Rome, rivers like roads.

Wood Cut

—from a fourteenth-century illustration

A woman in rough cloth nurses bears.
Though no witch, the black dots
of the nipples stare. Only one flows,
the other too ragged, but both
buzz beneath her skin when a beast
in shackles totters past:

pets of a German prince. To her
he feeds the best meats: sweet liver
and kidney, crooning *liebe, liebe,*
to the wet, nuzzling cub.
Her milk spurts a fountain.

She and her suckling grown huge
he makes to dance one winter's eve.
The lash coils at her ankles. Together,
they turn as bride and groom at festival.

Coins mount. The animal lurches
and she crumples, infuriating
his shaggy love. She dies and dies
at the bear's back. For an instant
her breast darkens the earth,
time enough for bees to gather.

As Told to Me

This year alone over fifty
head of cattle were found
dead of strange mutilations.
Locals fear an invasion
from space.
—*Kansas City Star*

She banked the pickup nose to nose
with another grey green hulk but
did not get out, just set the lights

low and yellow, just smiled.
Her hair stood from her head as
well-turned as a Texas cheerleader

but she kissed as if her cups cut.
Back at the cafe, he'd wondered
what they did in these towns.

Could take you on a tour,
she'd purred. Now, heaving him
off her, she slid out the door

into the ring of pickups. A peacock
advanced; she screamed with it.
Other women arrived, bending

in unison, looking like fungus
in their downfilled jackets,
leading a big animal. *What*

the hell? He thought he'd leave
but she had the keys. He could
only pop the locks down when

he saw her take something long and wet
into her lap, staining herself
as if from some overturned meal.

High School Rodeo Parade

It starts when the cop drops the wax paper
of his lunch and the clown zips closed his fly
and the youngster straps himself into his drum

and two girls, pre-pubescent enough so
their satin shorts are not too lascivious,
step out with the banner but not with

the music. Maybe the riff is too jazzy.
The old folks think so, collapsed
in their collapsible chairs, though the crowd,

two deep, applauds: the wood-block clap of men,
the cottonwood fluttering of women. Children
call out to siblings too embarrassed to wave.

On the first float, cavemen re-invent the wheel
and the new doctor reveals his legs. Covered
with makeup, no one smells paper scorching

from the motorcycles of the Optimists,
who, in sort of recompense, toss pennies.
Boys knock out their teeth scrambling for them,

looking up, bleeding, to see horses tall
as trees treading the coppers. Their riders
are nervous: anyone could dart out to stroke

a nose and these are cattle-cutters. An added hazard
is the cyclist, his one wheel weaving eights
around the horses' legs. How does he get on?

No adult knows. The fire engine and the ambulance
follow, the volunteers with their hats doffed
to resuscitate some plastic woman. *Feel her up*

steams one bystander. No one hears him, or pretends
so. Next, the single tank of the National Guard
revolves its muzzle like a drowning mole.

Brothers, cousins, fathers with helmets pulled
so low they can't see who they're marching to,
advance before the veterans whose drinks have worn off,

whose wives are leaving them, whose children go
to expensive schools. They're last because they've
marched before. When the street sweeper ends it, spinning

from gutter to gutter, whirring away the festive offal,
the people left stare across the suddenly empty street,
expectantly, as they never do.

Roundup

And I can hear my father's yahoo
and the hooves coming closer,
the herd heading for the gate
which is inexplicably open.

For a long time the horses
have known about it. They whinny
with their heads down. From under
their hooves the blank slight swell

of earth opens like an egg
cut with a knife. And I can hear
curses and the bulls' bodies
smashing into the missile

as it springs into place.
For a moment, all my father's
UFO fantasies are vindicated,
those culled from the prairie's

emptiness. A thrill of pride
winds up his gut, an intoxication
like the Sioux' who imagined
they owned all they could ride through.

But before it fires, a transparency
comes over us all: the cows against
the wedge of a daytime moon, all
four feet lifted, the rodeo trophies

in the bunkhouse showing their armatures,
my father's love for a woman other

than my mother apparent in the rounding
of her name in his throathole. Then

the buffaloes' thunder returns
just ahead of a great prairie fire
that wants grass six feet high,
what's left of the imagination.

The Contemporary Poetry Series
Edited by Paul Zimmer

The Contemporary Poetry Series

Edited by Bin Ramke